The Key Facts™ on

Azerbaijan

Essential Information on Azerbaijan

By Patrick W. Nee

The Internationalist®

www.internationalist.com

The Internationalist®

International Business, Investment, and Travel

Published by:

The Internationalist Publishing Company

96 Walter Street/ Suite 200

Boston, MA 02131, USA

Tel: 617-354-7722

www.internationalist.com

PN@internationalist.com

The Internationalist is a Registered Trademark. "Key Facts" and "The Internationalist Business Guides" are Trademarks of The Internationalist Publishing Company.

Table Of Contents

Chapter 1: Background

Azerbaijan - a nation with a majority-Turkic and majority-Shia Muslim population - was briefly independent (from 1918 to 1920) following the collapse of the Russian Empire; it was subsequently incorporated into the Soviet Union for seven decades. Azerbaijan has yet to resolve its conflict with Armenia over Nagorno-Karabakh, a primarily Armenian-populated region that Moscow recognized in 1923 as an autonomous republic within Soviet Azerbaijan after Armenia and Azerbaijan disputed the territory's status. Armenia and Azerbaijan began fighting over the area in 1988; the struggle escalated after both countries attained independence from the Soviet Union in 1991. By May 1994, when a cease-fire took hold, ethnic Armenian forces held not only Nagorno-Karabakh but also seven surrounding provinces in the territory of Azerbaijan. The OSCE Minsk Group, co-chaired by the United States, France, and Russia, is the framework established to mediate a peaceful resolution of the conflict. Corruption in the country is widespread, and the government, which eliminated presidential term limits in a 2009 referendum, has been accused of authoritarianism. Although the poverty rate has been reduced and infrastructure investment has increased substantially in recent years due to revenue from oil and gas production, reforms have not adequately addressed weaknesses in most government institutions, particularly in the education and health sectors.

Chapter 2: Geography

Location:

Southwestern Asia, bordering the Caspian Sea, between Iran and Russia, with a small European portion north of the Caucasus range

Geographic coordinates:

40 30 N, 47 30 E

Map references:

Middle East

Area:

total: 86,600 sq km

country comparison to the world: 113

land: 82,629 sq km

water: 3,971 sq km

note: includes the exclave of Naxcivan Autonomous Republic and the Nagorno-Karabakh region; the region's autonomy was abolished by Azerbaijani Supreme Soviet on 26 November 1991

Area - comparative:

slightly smaller than Maine

Land boundaries:

total: 2,013 km

border countries: Armenia (with Azerbaijan-proper) 566 km, Armenia (with Azerbaijan-Naxcivan exclave) 221 km, Georgia 322 km, Iran (with Azerbaijan-proper) 432 km, Iran (with Azerbaijan-Naxcivan exclave) 179 km, Russia 284 km, Turkey 9 km

Coastline:

0 km (landlocked); note - Azerbaijan borders the Caspian Sea (713 km)

Maritime claims:

none (landlocked)

Climate:

dry, semiarid steppe

Terrain:

large, flat Kur-Araz Ovaligi (Kura-Araks Lowland, much of it below sea level) with Great Caucasus Mountains to the north, Qarabag Yaylasi (Karabakh Upland) in west; Baku lies on Abseron Yasaqligi (Apsheron Peninsula) that juts into Caspian Sea

Elevation extremes:

lowest point: Caspian Sea -28 m

highest point: Bazarduzu Dagi 4,485 m

Natural resources:

petroleum, natural gas, iron ore, nonferrous metals, bauxite

Land use:

arable land: 21.78%

permanent crops: 2.62%

other: 75.6% (2011)

Irrigated land:

14,250 sq km (2010)

Total renewable water resources:

34.68 cu km (2011)

Freshwater withdrawal (domestic/industrial/agricultural):

total: 12.21 cu km/yr (4%/18%/78%)

per capita: 1,384 cu m/yr (2010)

Natural hazards:

droughts

Environment - current issues:

local scientists consider the Abseron Yasaqligi (Apsheron
Peninsula) (including Baku and Sumqayit) and the Caspian
Sea to be the ecologically most devastated area in the
world because of severe air, soil, and water pollution; soil
pollution results from oil spills, from the use of DDT
pesticide, and from toxic defoliants used in the production
of cotton

Environment - international agreements:

party to: Air Pollution, Biodiversity, Climate Change, Climate Change-Kyoto Protocol, Desertification, Endangered Species, Hazardous Wastes, Marine Dumping, Ozone Layer Protection, Ship Pollution, Wetlands

signed, but not ratified: none of the selected agreements

Geography - note:

both the main area of the country and the Naxcivan exclave are landlocked

Chapter 3: People and Society

Nationality:

noun: Azerbaijani(s)

adjective: Azerbaijani

Ethnic groups:

Azerbaijani 91.6%, Lezgian 2%, Russian 1.3%, Armenian 1.3%, Talysh 1.3%, other 2.4%

note: almost all Armenians live in the separatist Nagorno-Karabakh region (2009 est.)

Languages:

Azerbaijani (Azeri) (official) 92.5%, Russian 1.4%, Armenian 1.4%, other 4.7% (2009 est.)

Religions:

Muslim 93.4%, Russian Orthodox 2.5%, Armenian Orthodox 2.3%, other 1.8% (1995 est.)

note: religious affiliation is still nominal in Azerbaijan; percentages for actual practicing adherents are much lower

Population:

9,686,210 (July 2014 est.)

country comparison to the world: 92

Age structure:

0-14 years: 22.7% (male 1,176,438/female 1,017,926)

15-24 years: 17.5% (male 877,773/female 818,380)

25-54 years: 45.1% (male 2,127,239/female 2,236,520)

55-64 years: 6.3% (male 379,081/female 442,970)

65 years and over: 6.3% (male 232,297/female 377,586)

(2014 est.)

Dependency ratios:

total dependency ratio: 38.5 %

youth dependency ratio: 30.8 %

elderly dependency ratio: 7.8 %

potential support ratio: 12.9 (2013)

Median age:

total: 30.1 years

male: 28.5 years

female: 31.9 years (2014 est.)

Population growth rate:

0.99% (2014 est.)

country comparison to the world: 121

Birth rate:

16.96 births/1,000 population (2014 est.)

country comparison to the world: 111

Death rate:

7.09 deaths/1,000 population (2014 est.)

country comparison to the world: 129

Net migration rate:

0 migrant(s)/1,000 population (2014 est.)

country comparison to the world: 96

Urbanization:

urban population: 53.6% of total population (2011)

rate of urbanization: 1.64% annual rate of change (2010-15 est.)

Major urban areas - population:

BAKU (capital) 2.123 million (2011)

Sex ratio:

at birth: 1.12 male(s)/female

0-14 years: 1.16 male(s)/female

15-24 years: 1.07 male(s)/female

25-54 years: 0.95 male(s)/female

55-64 years: 0.98 male(s)/female

65 years and over: 0.62 male(s)/female

total population: 0.98 male(s)/female (2014 est.)

Mother's mean age at first birth:

24.4 (2010 est.)

Maternal mortality rate:

43 deaths/100,000 live births (2010)

country comparison to the world: 113

Infant mortality rate:

   total: 26.67 deaths/1,000 live births

   country comparison to the world: 69

   male: 27.47 deaths/1,000 live births

   female: 25.76 deaths/1,000 live births (2014 est.)

Life expectancy at birth:

   total population: 71.91 years

   country comparison to the world: 141

   male: 68.92 years

   female: 75.26 years (2014 est.)

Total fertility rate:

   1.91 children born/woman (2014 est.)

   country comparison to the world: 138

Contraceptive prevalence rate:

   51.1% (2006)

Health expenditures:

   5.2% of GDP (2011)

   country comparison to the world: 136

Physicians density:

   3.38 physicians/1,000 population (2011)

Hospital bed density:

   4.6 beds/1,000 population (2011)

Drinking water source:

improved:

urban: 88.4% of population

rural: 70.7% of population

total: 80.2% of population

unimproved:

urban: 11.6% of population

rural: 29.3% of population

total: 19.8% of population (2011 est.)

Sanitation facility access:

improved:

urban: 85.9% of population

rural: 77.5% of population

total: 82% of population

unimproved:

urban: 14.1% of population

rural: 22.5% of population

total: 18% of population (2011 est.)

HIV/AIDS - adult prevalence rate:

0.2% (2012 est.)

country comparison to the world: 106

HIV/AIDS - people living with HIV/AIDS:

10,400 (2012 est.)

country comparison to the world: 102

HIV/AIDS - deaths:

600 (2012 est.)

country comparison to the world: 85

Obesity - adult prevalence rate:

23.8% (2008)

country comparison to the world: 71

Children under the age of 5 underweight:

8.4% (2006)

country comparison to the world: 74

Education expenditures:

2.4% of GDP (2011)

country comparison to the world: 158

Literacy:

definition: age 15 and over can read and write

total population: 99.8%

male: 99.9%

female: 99.7% (2010 census)

School life expectancy (primary to tertiary education):

total: 12 years

male: 12 years

female: 12 years (2012)

Child labor – children ages 5-14:

total number: 106,626

percentage: 7 % (2005 est.)

Unemployment, youth ages 15-24:

> total: 14.6%
>
> country comparison to the world: 90
>
> male: 12.2%
>
> female: 16.3% (2012)

Chapter 4: Government and Key Leaders

Country name:

conventional long form: Republic of Azerbaijan

conventional short form: Azerbaijan

local long form: Azarbaycan Respublikasi

local short form: Azarbaycan

former: Azerbaijan Soviet Socialist Republic

Government type:

republic

Capital:

name: Baku (Baki, Baky)

geographic coordinates: 40 23 N, 49 52 E

time difference: UTC+4 (9 hours ahead of Washington, DC during Standard Time)

Administrative divisions:

66 rayons (rayonlar; rayon - singular), 11 cities (saharlar; sahar - singular);

rayons: Abseron, Agcabadi, Agdam, Agdas, Agstafa, Agsu, Astara, Babak, Balakan, Barda, Beylaqan, Bilasuvar, Cabrayil, Calilabad, Culfa, Daskasan, Fuzuli, Gadabay, Goranboy, Goycay, Goygol, Haciqabul, Imisli, Ismayilli, Kalbacar, Kangarli, Kurdamir, Lacin, Lankaran, Lerik, Masalli, Neftcala, Oguz, Ordubad, Qabala, Qax, Qazax, Qobustan, Quba, Qubadli, Qusar, Saatli, Sabirabad, Sabran, Sadarak, Sahbuz, Saki, Salyan, Samaxi, Samkir, Samux,

Sarur, Siyazan, Susa, Tartar, Tovuz, Ucar, Xacmaz, Xizi, Xocali, Xocavand, Yardimli, Yevlax, Zangilan, Zaqatala, Zardab

cities: Baku, Ganca, Lankaran, Mingacevir, Naftalan, Naxcivan (Nakhichevan), Saki, Sirvan, Sumqayit, Xankandi, Yevlax

Independence:

30 August 1991 (declared from the Soviet Union); 18 October 1991 (adopted by the Supreme Council of Azerbaijan)

National holiday:

Founding of the Democratic Republic of Azerbaijan, 28 May (1918)

Constitution:

several previous; latest adopted 12 November 1995; amended 1996, 2002, 2009 (2009)

Legal system:

civil law system

International law organization participation:

has not submitted an ICJ jurisdiction declaration; non-party state to the ICCt

Suffrage:

18 years of age; universal

Executive branch:

chief of state: President Ilham ALIYEV (since 31 October 2003) head of government: Prime Minister Artur RASIZADE (since 4 November 2003); First Deputy Prime Minister Yaqub EYYUBOV (since June 2006)

cabinet: Council of Ministers appointed by the president and confirmed by the National Assembly

elections: president elected by popular vote for a five-year term (eligible for unlimited terms); election last held on 9 October 2013 (next to be held in October 2018); prime minister and first deputy prime minister appointed by the president and confirmed by the National Assembly

election results: Ilham ALIYEV reelected president; percent of vote - Ilham ALIYEV 84.5%, Jamil HASANLI 5.5%, other 10%

note: OSCE observers concluded that the election did not meet international standards

Legislative branch:

unicameral National Assembly or Milli Mejlis (125 seats; members elected by popular vote to serve five-year terms)

elections: last held on 7 November 2010 (next to be held in November 2015)

election results: percent of vote by party - YAP 45.8%, CSP 1.6%, Motherland 1.4%, independents 48.2%, other 3.1%; seats by party - YAP 71, CSP 3, Motherland 2, Democratic Reforms 1, Great Creation 1, Hope Party 1, Social Welfare 1, Civil Unity 1, Whole Azerbaijan Popular Front 1, Justice 1, independents 42

Judicial branch:

Highest court(s): Supreme Court (consists of the chairman, deputy chairman, and at least 24 judges in plenum sessions); Constitutional Court (consists of 9 judges)

Judge selection and term of offfice: Supreme Court judges nominated by the president and appointed by the Milli Majlis; judge tenure NA; Constitutional Court chairman and deputy chairman appointed by the president; other court judges nominated by the president and appointed by the Milli Majlis to serve single 15-year terms

subordinate courts: Courts of Appeal (replaced the Economic Court in 2002); district and municipal courts;

Political parties and leaders:

Azerbaijan Democratic Party or ADP [Sardar JALALOGLU]

Azerbaijan Popular Front or AXCP [Ali KARIMLI]

Civil Solidarity Party or CSP [Sabir RUSTAMKHANLI]

Civil Unity Party [Sabir HACIYEV]

Classical Popular Front Party of Azerbaijan [Mirmahmud MIRALI-OGLU]

Democratic Reforms Party [Asim MOLLAZADE]

Great Creation Party [Fazil Gazanfaroglu MUSTAFAYEV]

Hope (Umid) Party [Igbal AGAZADE]

Justice Party [Ilyas ISMAILOV]

Liberal Party of Azerbaijan [Lala Shovkat HACIYEVA, Avaz TEMIRKHAN]

Motherland Party [Fazail AGAMALI]

Musavat (Equality) [Isa GAMBAR]

Open Society Party [Sulhaddin AKBAR]

Social Democratic Party of Azerbaijan or SDP [Araz ALIZADE]

Social Welfare Party [Khanhusein KAZIMLI]

Whole Azerbaijan Popular Front Party [Gudrat HASANGULIYEV]

Yeni (New) Azerbaijan Party or YAP [President Ilham ALIYEV]

Political pressure groups and leaders:

EL Movement [Eldar NAMAZOV]

Karabakh Liberation Organization

Forum of Intelligentsia [Rustam IBRAHIMBEYOV]

Republican Alternative (REAL) [Ilgar MAMMADOV]

National Council of Democratic Forces [Jamil HASANLI]

NIDA Youth Movement [Turgut GAMBAR, Zaur GURBANLI (in jail)]

Positive Change Youth Movement [Bakhtiyar HAJIYEV]

Ireli Youth Movement [Rauf MERDIYEV]

Ol! Youth Movement [Vugar SALAMLI]

International organization participation:

ADB, BSEC, CD, CE, CICA, CIS, EAPC, EBRD, ECO, EITI (compliant country), FAO, GCTU, GUAM, IAEA, IBRD, ICAO, ICC (NGOs), ICRM, IDA, IDB, IFAD, IFC, IFRCS, ILO, IMF, IMO, Interpol, IOC, IOM, IPU, ISO, ITSO, ITU, ITUC (NGOs), MIGA, NAM, OAS (observer), OIC, OPCW, OSCE, PFP, SELEC (observer), UN, UNCTAD, UNESCO, UNHCR, UNIDO, UNWTO, UPU, WCO, WFTU (NGOs), WHO, WIPO, WMO, WTO (observer)

Diplomatic representation in the US:

chief of mission: Ambassador Elin SULEYMANOV (since 5 December 2011)

chancery: 2741 34th Street NW, Washington, DC 20008

telephone: [1] (202) 337-3500

FAX: [1] (202) 337-5911

consulate(s) general: Los Angeles

Diplomatic representation from the US:

chief of mission: Ambassador Richard L. MORNINGSTAR (since 20 July 2012)

embassy: 111 Azadlig Prospecti, Baku AZ1007

mailing address: American Embassy Baku, US Department of State, 7050 Baku Place, Washington, DC 20521-7050

telephone: [994] (12) 488-3300

FAX: [994] (12) 488-3310

Key Leaders:

Pres.	Ilham ALIYEV
Prime Min.	Artur RASIZADE
First Dep. Prime Min.	Yaqub EYYUBOV
Dep. Prime Min.	Ismat ABBASOV
Dep. Prime Min.	Ali AKHMEDOV
Dep. Prime Min.	Elchin EFENDIYEV
Dep. Prime Min.	Ali HASANOV
Dep. Prime Min.	Abid SHARIFOV
Min. of Agriculture	Heydar ASADOV
Min. of Communications & Information Technology	Ali ABBASOV
Min. of Culture & Tourism	Abulfaz GARAYEV
Min. of Defense	Zakir HASANOV, *Col. Gen.*
Min. of Defense Industry	Yavar JAMALOV
Min. of Ecology & Natural Resources	Huseyngulu BAGIROV

Min. of Economy & Industry	Shahin MUSTAFAYEV
Min. of Education	Mikayil JABBAROV
Min. of Emergency Situations	Kamaladdin HEYDAROV
Min. of Energy	Natiq ALIYEV
Min. of Finance	Samir SHARIFOV
Min. of Foreign Affairs	Elmar MAMMADYAROV
Min. of Health	Oqtay SHIRALIYEV
Min. of Internal Affairs	Ramil USUBOV, *Col. Gen.*
Min. of Justice	Fikret MAMEDOV
Min. of Labor & Social Security	Salim MUSLUMOV
Min. of National Security	Eldar MAHMUDOV
Min. of Sports & Youth	Azad RAHIMOV
Min. of Taxation	Fazil MAMEDOV
Min. of Transport	Ziya MAMMADOV
Chmn., National Bank	Elman RUSTAMOV
Ambassador to the US	Elin SULEYMANOV
Permanent Representative to the UN, New York	Agshin MEHDIYEV

Flag description:

three equal horizontal bands of blue (top), red, and green; a crescent and eight-pointed star in white are centered in the red band; the blue band recalls Azerbaijan's Turkic heritage, red stands for modernization and progress, and green refers to Islam; the crescent moon is an Islamic symbol, while the eight-pointed star represents the eight Turkic peoples of the world

National symbol(s):

flames of fire

National anthem:

name: "Azerbaijan Marsi" (March of Azerbaijan)

lyrics/music: Ahmed JAVAD/Uzeyir HAJIBEYOV

note: adopted 1992; although originally written in 1919 during a brief period of independence, "Azerbaijan Marsi" did not become the official anthem until after the dissolution of the Soviet Union

Chapter 5: Economy

Economy - overview:

Azerbaijan's high economic growth has been attributable to large and growing oil and gas exports, but some non-export sectors also featured double-digit growth, including construction, banking, and real estate. Oil exports through the Baku-Tbilisi-Ceyhan Pipeline, the Baku-Novorossiysk, and the Baku-Supsa pipelines remain the main economic driver, but efforts to boost Azerbaijan's gas production are underway. The eventual completion of the geopolitically important Southern Gas Corridor between Azerbaijan and Europe will open up another, albeit, smaller source of revenue from gas exports. Azerbaijan has made only limited progress on instituting market-based economic reforms. Pervasive public and private sector corruption and structural economic inefficiencies remain a drag on long-term growth, particularly in non-energy sectors. Several other obstacles impede Azerbaijan's economic progress, including the need for stepped up foreign investment in the non-energy sector and the continuing conflict with Armenia over the Nagorno-Karabakh region. Trade with Russia and the other former Soviet republics is declining in importance, while trade is building with Turkey and the nations of Europe. Long-term prospects depend on world oil prices, Azerbaijan's ability to negotiate export routes for its growing gas production, and its ability to use its energy wealth to promote growth and spur employment in non-energy sectors of the economy.

GDP (purchasing power parity):

$100.4 billion (2013 est.)

country comparison to the world: 76

$97.04 billion (2012 est.)

$94.98 billion (2011 est.)

note: data are in 2013 US dollars

GDP (official exchange rate):

$76.01 billion (2013 est.)

GDP - real growth rate:

3.5% (2013 est.)

country comparison to the world: 96

2.2% (2012 est.)

0.1% (2011 est.)

GDP - per capita (PPP):

$10,800 (2013 est.)

country comparison to the world: 114

$10,500 (2012 est.)

$10,400 (2011 est.)

note: data are in 2013 US dollars

Gross national saving:

41% of GDP (2013 est.)

country comparison to the world: 10

44.4% of GDP (2012 est.)

45.1% of GDP (2011 est.)

GDP – composition, by end use:

household consumption: 41.4%

government consumption: 10.5%

investment in fixed capital: 23.3%

investment in inventories: 0.1%

exports of goods and services: 49.9%

imports of goods and services: -25.2% (2013 est.)

GDP - composition by sector:

agriculture: 6.2%

industry: 63%

services: 30.8% (2013 est.)

Agriculture – products:

cotton, grain, rice, grapes, fruit, vegetables, tea, tobacco;
cattle, pigs, sheep, goats

Industries:

petroleum and natural gas, petroleum products, oilfield
equipment; steel, iron ore; cement; chemicals and
petrochemicals; textiles

Industrial production growth rate:

3% (2013 est.)

country comparison to the world: 107

Labor force:

6.206 million (2012 est.)

country comparison to the world: 66

Labor force - by occupation:

agriculture: 38.3%

industry: 12.1%

services: 49.6% (2008)

Unemployment rate:

6% (2013 est.)

country comparison to the world: 58

5.7% (2012 est.)

Population below poverty line:

6% (2012 est.)

Household income or consumption by percentage share:

lowest 10%: 3.4%

highest 10%: 27.4% (2008)

Distribution of family income - Gini index:

33.7 (2008)

country comparison to the world: 97

36.5 (2001)

Budget:

revenues: $27.61 billion

expenditures: $27.24 billion (2013 est.)

Taxes and other revenues:

36.3% of GDP (2013 est.)

country comparison to the world: 59

Budget surplus (+) or deficit (-):

0.5% of GDP (2013 est.)

country comparison to the world: 33

Public Debt:

7.5% of GDP (2013 est.)

country comparison to the world: 152

7.8% of GDP (2012 est.)

Inflation rate (consumer prices):

2.4% (2013 est.)

country comparison to the world: 87

1.1% (2012 est.)

Central bank discount rate:

5% (31 December 2012 est.)

country comparison to the world: 67

5.25% (31 December 2011 est.)

note: this is the Refinancing Rate, the key policy rate for the National Bank of Azerbaijan

Commercial bank prime lending rate:

17% (31 December 2013 est.)

country comparison to the world: 21

18.5% (31 December 2012 est.)

Stock of narrow money:

$17.17 billion (31 December 2013 est.)

country comparison to the world: 67

$14.15 billion (31 December 2012 est.)

Stock of broad money:

$21.88 billion (31 December 2013 est.)

country comparison to the world: 83

$17.59 billion (31 December 2012 est.)

Stock of domestic credit:

$21.76 billion (31 December 2013 est.)

country comparison to the world: 82

$17.01 billion (31 December 2012 est.)

Current account balance:

$13.28 billion (2013 est.)

country comparison to the world: 20

$14.98 billion (2012 est.)

Exports:

$34.46 billion (2013 est.)

country comparison to the world: 63

$32.63 billion (2012 est.)

Exports - commodities:

oil and gas 90%, machinery, cotton, foodstuffs

Exports - partners:

Italy 27.1%, France 8.1%, Indonesia 6.9%, Germany 5.9%, Israel 5.4%, India 4.2%, US 4.2% (2012)

Imports:

$11.98 billion (2013 est.)

country comparison to the world: 94

$10.42 billion (2012 est.)

Imports - commodities:

machinery and equipment, oil products, foodstuffs, metals, chemicals

Imports - partners:

Turkey 17.8%, Russia 13.7%, China 7.5%, Germany 6.9%, UK 6.8%, Ukraine 5.5%, US 4.9% (2012)

Reserves of foreign exchange and gold:

$13.08 billion (31 December 2013 est.)

country comparison to the world: 70

$11.28 billion (31 December 2012 est.)

Debt - external:

$9.552 billion (31 December 2013 est.)

country comparison to the world: 101

$9.11 billion (31 December 2012 est.)

Stock of direct foreign investment – at home:

$14.35 billion (31 December 2013 est.)

country comparison to the world: 82

$12.35 billion (31 December 2012 est.)

Stock of direct foreign investment – abroad:

$8.616 billion (31 December 2013 est.)

country comparison to the world: 57

$7.516 billion (31 December 2012 est.)

Exchange rates:

Azerbaijani manats (AZN) per US dollar -

0.785 (2013 est.)

0.7857 (2012 est.)

0.8027 (2010 est.)

0.8038 (2009)

0.8219 (2008)

Chapter 6: Energy

Electricity - production:

    19.44 billion kWh (2011 est.)

    country comparison to the world: 75

Electricity - consumption:

    13.57 billion kWh (2010 est.)

    country comparison to the world: 80

Electricity - exports:

    462 million kWh (2010 est.)

    country comparison to the world: 66

Electricity - imports:

    100 million kWh (2010 est.)

    country comparison to the world: 93

Electricity - installed generating capacity:

    6.392 million kW (2010 est.)

    country comparison to the world: 70

Electricity - from fossil fuels:

    84.5% of total installed capacity (2010 est.)

    country comparison to the world: 89

Electricity - from nuclear fuels:

    0% of total installed capacity (2010 est.)

    country comparison to the world: 36

Electricity - from hydroelectric plants:

    15.4% of total installed capacity (2010 est.)

    country comparison to the world: 100

Electricity - from other renewable sources:

0.1% of total installed capacity (2010 est.)

country comparison to the world: 105

Crude oil - production:

931,900 bbl/day (2012 est.)

country comparison to the world: 25

Crude oil - exports:

821,000 bbl/day (2011 est.)

country comparison to the world: 17

Crude oil - imports:

0 bbl/day (2010 est.)

country comparison to the world: 150

Crude oil - proved reserves:

7 billion bbl (1 January 2013 es)

country comparison to the world: 20

Refined petroleum products - production:

133,500 bbl/day (2010 est.)

country comparison to the world: 65

Refined petroleum products - consumption:

168,000 bbl/day (2011 est.)

country comparison to the world: 63

Refined petroleum products - exports:

53,440 bbl/day (2010 est.)

country comparison to the world: 60

Refined petroleum products - imports:

498.6 bbl/day (2010 est.)

country comparison to the world: 204

Natural gas - production:

17.86 billion cu m (2011 est.)

country comparison to the world: 34

Natural gas - consumption:

9.921 billion cu m (2010 est.)

country comparison to the world: 47

Natural gas - exports:

5.55 billion cu m (2011 est.)

country comparison to the world: 33

Natural gas - imports:

250 million cu m (2011 est.)

country comparison to the world: 70

Natural gas - proved reserves:

991.1 billion cu m (1 January 2013 es)

country comparison to the world: 28

Carbon dioxide emissions from consumption of energy:

36.52 million Mt (2011 est.)

country comparison to the world: 73

Chapter 7: Communications

Telephones - main lines in use:

> 1.734 million (2012)

> country comparison to the world: 64

Telephones - mobile cellular:

> 10.125 million (2012)

> country comparison to the world: 78

Telephone system:

> general assessment: requires considerable expansion and modernization; fixed-line telephone and a broad range of other telecom services are controlled by a state-owned telecommunications monopoly and growth has been stagnant; more competition exists in the mobile-cellular market with four providers in 2009

> domestic: teledensity of 17 fixed lines per 100 persons; mobile-cellular teledensity has increased and now exceeds 100 telephones per 100 persons; satellite service connects Baku to a modern switch in its exclave of Naxcivan (Nakhichevan)

> international: country code - 994; the Trans-Asia-Europe (TAE) fiber-optic link transits Azerbaijan providing international connectivity to neighboring countries; the old Soviet system of cable and microwave is still serviceable; satellite earth stations - 2 (2011)

Broadcast media:

3 state-run and 1 public TV channels; 4 domestic commercial TV stations and about 15 regional TV stations; cable TV services are available in Baku; 1 state-run and 1 public radio network operating; a small number of private commercial radio stations broadcasting; local FM relays of Baku commercial stations are available in many localities; local relays of several international broadcasters had been available until late 2008 when their broadcasts were banned from FM frequencies (2010)

Internet country code:

.az

Internet hosts:

46,856 (2012)

country comparison to the world: 98

Internet users:

2.42 million (2009)

country comparison to the world: 70

Chapter 8: Transportation

Airports:

    37 (2013)

    country comparison to the world: 108

Airports - with paved runways:

    total: 30

    over 3,047 m: 5

    2,438 to 3,047 m: 5

    1,524 to 2,437 m: 13

    914 to 1,523 m: 4

    under 914 m: 3 (2013)

Airports - with unpaved runways:

    total: 7

    under 914 m: 7 (2013)

Heliports:

    1 (2012)

Pipelines:

    condensate 89 km; gas 3,890 km; oil 2,446 km (2013)

Railways:

    total: 2,918 km

    country comparison to the world: 58

    broad gauge: 2,918 km 1.520-m gauge (1,278 km electrified) (2009)

Roadways:

total: 52,942 km

country comparison to the world: 75

paved: 26,789 km

unpaved: 26,153 km (2006)

Merchant marine:

total: 90

country comparison to the world: 53

by type: cargo 27, chemical tanker 1, passenger 2,

passenger/cargo 8, petroleum tanker 47, roll on/roll off 3,

specialized tanker 2

foreign-owned: 1 (Turkey 1)

registered in other countries: 2 (Malta 1, Saint Vincent and

the Grenadines 1) (2010)

Ports and terminals:

major seaport(s): Baku (Baki) located on the Caspian Sea

Chapter 9: Military

Military branches:

Army, Navy, Air, and Air Defense Forces (2010)

Military service age and obligation:

men between 18 and 35 are liable for military service; length of service is 18 months and 12 months for university graduates; 17 years of age for voluntary service; 17 year olds are considered to be on active service at cadet military schools (2012)

Manpower available for military service:

males age 16-49: 2,354,249

females age 16-49: 2,334,632 (2010 est.)

Manpower fit for military service:

males age 16-49: 1,773,993

females age 16-49: 1,964,012 (2010 est.)

Manpower reaching militarily significant age annually:

male: 76,923

female: 71,024 (2010 est.)

Military expenditures:

5.2% of GDP (2013)

country comparison to the world: 5

4.64% of GDP (2012)

4.67% of GDP (2011)

4.64% of GDP (2010)

Chapter 10: Transnational Issues

Disputes - international:

Azerbaijan, Kazakhstan, and Russia ratified the Caspian seabed delimitation treaties based on equidistance, while Iran continues to insist on a one-fifth slice of the sea; the dispute over the break-away Nagorno-Karabakh region and the Armenian military occupation of surrounding lands in Azerbaijan remains the primary focus of regional instability; residents have evacuated the former Soviet-era small ethnic enclaves in Armenia and Azerbaijan; local border forces struggle to control the illegal transit of goods and people across the porous, undemarcated Armenian, Azerbaijani, and Georgian borders; bilateral talks continue with Turkmenistan on dividing the seabed and contested oilfields in the middle of the Caspian

Refugees and internally displaced persons:

IDPs: 597,429 (conflict with Armenia over Nagorno-Karabakh; IDPs are mainly ethnic Azerbaijanis but also include ethnic Kurds, Russians, and Turks predominantly from occupied territories around Nagorno-Karabakh; number includes IDPs' descendants, returned IDPs, and people living in insecure areas and excludes people displaced by natural disasters; around half the IDPs live in the capital Baku) (2014)

stateless persons: 3,585 (2012)

Illicit drugs:

limited illicit cultivation of cannabis and opium poppy, mostly for CIS consumption; small government eradication program; transit point for Southwest Asian opiates bound for Russia and to a lesser extent the rest of Europe

Map of Azerbaijan

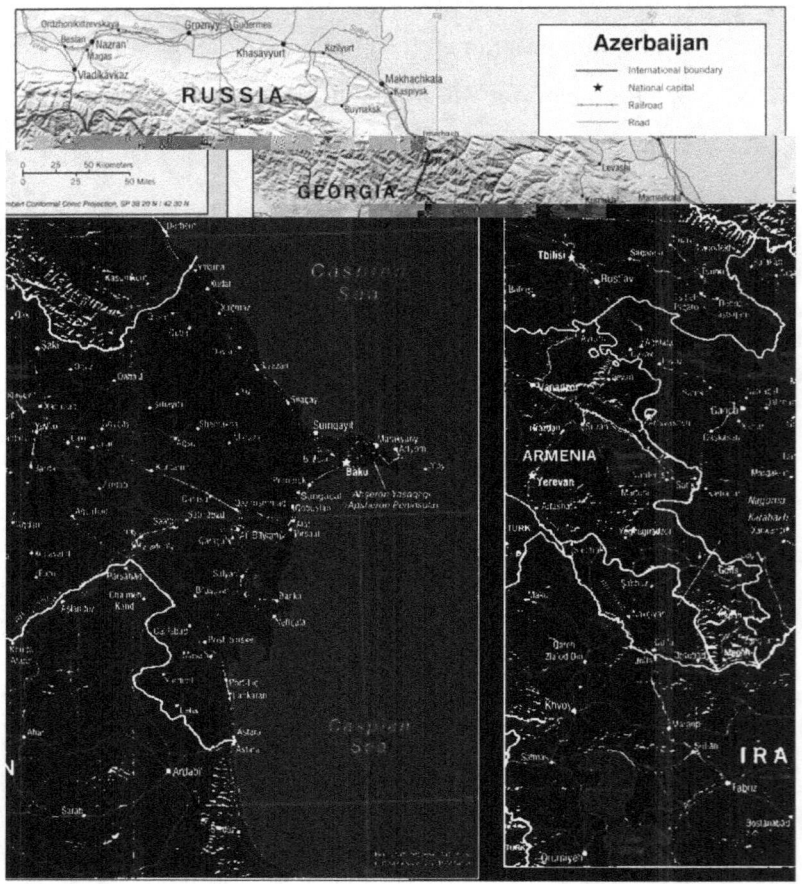

Other Key Facts™ Titles

Key Facts on South Korea

Key Facts on France

Key Facts on the United Kingdom

Key Facts on Egypt

Key Facts on Israel

All Key Facts™ Titles are Available at

www.Amazon.com

THE INTERNATIONALIST®

2014

WWW.INTERNATIONALIST.COM